DWAYNE JOHNSON

BY JEN JONES

CAPSTONE PRESS
a capstone imprint

Edge Books are published by Capstone Press,
1710 Roe Crest Drive, North Mankato, Minnesota 56003
www.mycapstone.com

Library of Congress Cataloging-in-Publication Data
Names: Jones, Jen, author.
Title: Dwayne Johnson / by Jen Jones.
Description: North Mankato, Minnesota : Capstone Press, 2017. | Series: Edge
  books: Hollywood action heroes | Includes bibliographical references and
  index.
Identifiers: LCCN 2016004948| ISBN 9781515710967 (library binding) | ISBN
  9781515712961 (ebook)
Subjects: LCSH: Johnson, Dwayne, 1972—Juvenile literature. |
  Wrestlers—United States—Biography--Juvenile literature. | Actors—United
  States—Biography--Juvenile literature.
Classification: LCC GV1196.J64 D66 2017 | DDC 796.812092--dc23
LC record available at http://lccn.loc.gov/2016004948

Editorial Credits
Linda Staniford, editor; Kyle Grenz, designer;
Eric Gohl, media researcher; Gene Bentdahl, production specialist

Photo Credits
Alamy: AF Archive, 15, Moviestore Collection Ltd, 17, 25, Photos 12, 21; AP
Photo: WWE/Jonathan Bachman, 29; Getty Images: Collegiate Images, 9,
George Pimentel, 10, Russell Turiak, 13; Newscom: Album/John Bramley/
Visual Arts Enter/Original Film/Columbia Pictures Industries, 18–19, Album/
Original Film, 22–23, Album/Paramount Pictures, 5, Hutchins Photo/Kathy
Hutchins, 7, iPhoto Inc./Greg Henkenhaf, 12; Shutterstock: Helga Esteb, 26, 27,
Tinseltown, cover, 1

Design Elements: Shutterstock

Printed in China.
042016   007737

TABLE OF CONTENTS

Lights, Camera, Action!

To wrestling fans, he's "The Rock." To movie buffs, he's simply Dwayne Johnson. He's a superstar who conquered the wrestling ring and is breaking the box office.

Towering at 6 feet 5 inches (2 meters) tall, Dwayne is a larger-than-life presence in more ways than one. His strong build and natural charm have helped him become a huge star and an in-demand action hero. The *Hollywood Reporter* once said he had the "wit of Willis, the strength of Schwarzenegger, and the heart of Stallone." To date, Dwayne's films have pulled in a total of $3.7 billion.

This guy's personality and entertaining antics can drive crowds crazy. And he doesn't plan on stopping any time soon. "What do I want?" Dwayne has said. "I want the world."

Dwayne as Roadblock in *G.I. Joe*

Chapter 2

Laying the Foundation

On May 2, 1972, a superstar was born. Future wrestling and acting sensation Dwayne Douglas Johnson was born in Hayward, California, to parents Rocky and Ata. One look at his family tree shows that Dwayne was **destined** to become a wrestler. His dad was a pro wrestler in the 1970s and 1980s. His grandfather, Peter Maivia, was also a wrestling legend. Nicknamed "The Flying Hawaiian," Peter won championships in the World Tag Team and National Wrestling Alliance (NWA). After his death Peter was entered into the World Wrestling Entertainment (WWE) Hall of Fame. On top of that, Dwayne's grandmother was a wrestling promoter, and several relatives have also been involved in the sport.

destined—meant to be or do something

Some of Dwayne's earliest memories include going to wrestling shows with his mom. His dad performed tricks like flying off the top rope of the ring. Dwayne was so inspired that he often practiced dropkicks in the living room. Later in life, these moves would come in handy—as Dwayne became one of wrestling's biggest stars of all time.

Dwayne's parents Ata (left) and Rocky (right) have always been very supportive of his career.

Fast Fact

Dwayne "The Rock" Johnson was the World Wrestling Federation's (WWF's) first third-generation wrestler.

Pigskin Prowess

Long before Dwayne was laying the smackdown, he was scoring touchdowns. When he was 16, his family moved to Pennsylvania. Dwayne's football career started at Freedom High School. He was ranked as one of Pennsylvania's top eight players. Dwayne was also named to *USA Today*'s All-American team.

After graduating high school in 1990, Dwayne earned a full football scholarship to the University of Miami in Florida. In 1991 he helped lead the Hurricanes to a national championship. However, a back injury during Dwayne's senior year sidelined his dreams of playing in the National Football League (NFL). Dwayne did later join the Calgary Stampeders in the Canadian Football League (CFL). To his disappointment, he was cut from the team just two months later. It was time to hang up the football jersey and see what else life held in store.

Dwayne wore the #94 jersey for the University of Miami Hurricanes. Here he tackles a Pittsburgh Panthers lineman.

In 1995, with just $7 to his name, Dwayne moved to Florida to be near his parents. Hoping to find a new career path, Dwayne asked his dad to teach him all about wrestling. Little did Dwayne know that he'd soon become a major force in the wrestling world.

Chapter 3

Making Moves

Even with an impressive family history, it's not easy for an unknown to break into pro wrestling. But Dwayne somehow pulled it off with flying colors. In 1996 he scored a WWF tryout and defeated "The Brooklyn Brawler." Within months of being signed, Dwayne defeated the experienced wrestler "Triple H" to win the Intercontinental Belt. He also won the "New Sensation" Slammy Award.

Dwayne "The Rock" Johnson was one of the top wrestling stars in Wrestlemania X8 in 2002.

Meet the Rock

All of these achievements happened for Dwayne in just over a year after his football career ended. But as his success climbed, audiences began booing him. Fans in the 1990s wanted over-the-top "villains." Dwayne's nice guy image just wasn't cutting it. It was time for a new approach. What emerged was "The Rock" —a tough-as-nails, tattooed bad boy in black boots. This **persona** would push him into the spotlight and mark the start of his **blockbuster** career.

persona—a character or personality

blockbuster—something that is very effective, successful, expensive, large, or extravagant

Fast Fact

Dwayne went by the names "Flex Kavana" and "Rocky Maivia" before settling on his famous nickname, "The Rock."

The People's Champion

Reinvented as "The Rock," it didn't take long for Dwayne to reach the top of the wrestling heap. Dwayne was part of wrestling's "Attitude Era," where **trash-talking** and shock value were the name of the game. Fans went crazy for "The Rock's" catchphrases. Two favorites were: "Can you smell what 'The Rock' is cooking?" and "Know your role, and shut your mouth!"

trash-talking—boastful talk used to threaten opponents

Dwyane wrestles Christian Cage at the Raw is War event in Toronto, Canada, 2001

"The Rock" came up against other icons like "Stone Cold" Steve Austin and "Mankind." His signature moves included "The People's Eyebrow" (a menacing eyebrow raise) and the "Rock Bottom" body slam. Over time, Dwayne racked up seven WWE championships, five World Tag Team championships, and two Intercontinental Championships. These wins made him a true "triple threat" as one of the few Triple Crown Champions in the sport.

> "'The Rock' is Dwayne Johnson with the volume turned all the way up."

–Dwayne on his Rock persona

13

Chapter 4

A New Direction

Once "The Rock" became a household name, Hollywood began to take notice. His popularity led to invitations to be in a Wyclef Jean music video and on the TV show *Star Trek: Voyager*. Dwayne even played his own father, Rocky Johnson, on *That '70s Show*. He also appeared in several TV movies, playing himself as "The Rock."

The doors to stardom were really thrown open for Dwayne when he hosted *Saturday Night Live* in 2000. Cracking jokes with Jimmy Fallon and Tina Fey, Dwayne proved he could command attention off the mat. After that night, his phone started ringing with offers from movie studios. Like superstar Hulk Hogan before him, "The Rock" was set to dominate once again—this time as an actor.

> *"Saturday Night Live ... gave me an opportunity to showcase my skill and broke me in terms of my career."*
>
> —Dwayne on his big break into showbiz

In an episode of *Star Trek: Voyager*, Dwayne played an alien who took on a member of the *Voyager* crew in a wrestling match.

It's Good to be King

In 2001 Dwayne landed his first movie role in *The Mummy Returns*. His powerful performance earned him a Teen Choice Award.

Dwayne's success in his first film led to an exciting offer to be the lead actor in the **prequel**, *The Scorpion King* (2002). Dwayne played a fierce desert warrior. The warrior's mission is to stop an evil king from wiping out his homeland and its people. Filled with fights and swordplay, the action-packed movie was the perfect way for "The Rock" to make the leap to movies.

prequel—a story about events that happen to characters before they appear in an existing story

Fast Fact

In the final battle scene of *The Scorpion King*, things got a little too heated. While fighting co-star Steven Brand with flaming swords, Dwayne almost burned his eyebrows off! The scene also featured one of Dwayne's trusty wrestling moves, a "kip-up". From lying down on the ground, he flips his body to standing up using his legs and core strength.

All of Dwayne's hard work paid off. He was paid $5.5 million for his role in *The Scorpion King*. It set a Guinness World Record for the highest salary for a first-time leading man.

Dwayne plays warrior Mathayus, who defeats his enemies to become the Scorpion King.

Worlds Colliding

Dwayne's football career ended with a thud several years before. However, his movie roles gave him the chance to revisit his passion for pigskin.

In **Gridiron** *Gang* (2006), Dwayne plays Sean Porter. His character helps troubled youth by forming a football team at a juvenile detention center. The movie was based on a true story. It was shot at the same place it was inspired, Camp Kilpatrick.

gridiron—a football field with evenly spaced lines

Football gives the kids in *Gridiron Gang* a new hope for the future.

Fast Fact

In a nod to his University of Miami days, Dwayne wears a #94 jersey in a *Gridiron Gang* practice scene.

The next year, *The Game Plan* (2007) allowed Dwayne to suit up once more. He portrayed an NFL player who learns that he has an 8-year-old daughter. He takes her under his wing and learns to become a loving father. Dwayne has said that this was the movie he had the most fun shooting. Not only was it was his first big comedy, but it also fulfilled his "dream of playing a professional quarterback."

Chapter 5

Non-stop Action

What better way to get respect as an action star than to play some of history's most famous heroes? With *G.I. Joe: Retaliation* (2013) and *Hercules* (2014), Dwayne did just that.

Anyone who knows the *G.I. Joe* universe knows about "Roadblock." Dwayne brought the tough-as-nails character to life in *G.I. Joe: Retaliation*. As the team's heavy machine gunner, Dwayne threw himself into the role. His elbows bled as he crawled through the desert during stunt scenes.

Playing Greek **demi-god** Hercules was also no easy feat. To build up his body for the role, Dwayne went on a 22-week power diet. He ate up to seven full meals a day with high-protein foods like steak, egg whites, fish, and broccoli. He even joked that he would drink "one cup of lion blood" every morning.

demi-god—a mythological being who is partly human and partly divine

To bulk up Dwayne also did heavy physical training. He worked out six days a week for six months. Once filming wrapped, Dwayne was proud of his hard work: "We've put a lot of blood, sweat, and tears into this movie."

"I had a massive collection of *G.I. Joe* and *Star Wars* action figures, and because I was an only child, they were my family and my friends."

—Dwayne on action heroes

Dwayne plays Roadblock, one of the *G.I. Joe* team that defeats terrorist organization COBRA in the movie.

Life in the "Fast" Lane

The *Fast & Furious* series has always attracted an army of loyal fans. But when Dwayne came on board for the fifth movie, *Fast Five* (2011), it gave the series a jolt of new life. Opening weekend pulled in $86.2 million, setting records for both Dwayne's movies and the *Fast* **franchise**.

franchise—a series of films or TV shows that feature the same characters or follow a continuing storyline

Dwayne can thank social media for the career-changing opportunity. His role was meant to go to an older actor. However, a fan's comment about wanting to see Vin Diesel take on "The Rock" changed everything. Enter DSS special agent Luke Hobbs, who drives a 10-ton, **armored** Gurkha truck. Director Justin Lin said that next to Dwayne, "anything less would look silly, like a clown car."

Fast Five's huge success led to Dwayne's return for the sixth and seventh *Fast & Furious* movies. Now he's part of what Vin Diesel calls the "family of misfits."

armored—covered with metal to protect against attacks

Dwayne plays Luke Hobbs, a Security Service agent who is trying to bring down a group of wanted criminals.

Shaking Things Up

Imagine an earthquake strong enough to break California in half. That's the plot of 2015's *San Andreas*, in which Dwayne plays a helicopter rescue pilot.

From the very first shot, Dwayne is in amped-up action hero mode. The opening scene features a girl whose car is teetering off the edge of a cliff. Dwayne's character must swoop in and save her, and not with fancy special effects. Instead, he had to dangle 150 feet (46 meters) out of a helicopter to do so. The director wanted the actors to do their own stunts so the audience could see their faces. "This isn't a trick. There's no editing," he said. "This is Dwayne really doing it."

That's not to say there was no movie magic in the film. More than 1,300 special effects were shot in the air, underground, and underwater. Dwayne filmed many scenes in a giant tank filled with more than 2 million gallons (9 million liters) of water. It's all in a day's work for this action hero!

In San Andreas Dwayne plays helicopter rescue pilot Ray Gaines.

Chapter 6

What's Dwayne Got Cooking?

Dwayne is one big guy with the heart to match. He devotes much of his time to good causes, especially those that help children in need. His Dwayne Johnson Rock Foundation works to help sick or disadvantaged youth. On the 2014 TNT reality show *Wake-Up Call,* Dwayne mentored a group of adult "everyday heroes." He helped them rise above challenges like dropping out of high school and saving a failing business.

Dwayne adds his handprints to those of many other Hollywood stars at the Forecourt of the Stars on Hollywood Boulevard in 2015.

When not saving the world or shooting movies, Dwayne's got plenty of hobbies to keep him busy. He can often be found hitting the water to go fishing. Early in 2015, he even nabbed a 200-pound (91-kilogram) tarpon! Dwayne also likes to show off his silly side. In 2014 he surprised crowds at a Hollywood comedy club with a hilarious stand-up routine. There's rarely a dull moment when "The Rock" is around!

Rock Solid

In 2013 Dwayne's movies were the highest **grossing** films in the world, bringing in $1.3 billion. Looking ahead, he has no fewer than eight movies in the hopper! Dwayne has also returned to the wrestling ring for special events. In WrestleMania 29 in 2013, his **bout** with John Cena attracted more than 80,000 WWE fans to New Jersey's MetLife Stadium. In 2014 he joined forces with Hulk Hogan and "Stone Cold" Steve Austin to kick off WrestleMania 30.

Dwayne Johnson's star power isn't going to dim any time soon. He always seems to have a new move up his sleeve. Wrestling star or action movie hero, his fans are eager to see what he will do next.

grossing—earning or bringing in money

bout—a contest or trial of strength, such as a wrestling or boxing match

Fast Fact

"The Rock" is huge on social media, too. He has tens of millions of followers. In May 2015, he broke a world record by taking 105 selfies in three minutes!

"I want to do more in the [WWE]. I want to do more in the movie industry. Ultimately, I want to be the most electrifying man in sports entertainment, period."

—Dwayne on his future career

JUST BRING IT

Dwayne appears regularly at Wrestlemania. Here he is at the 2014 event, wearing a shirt with his slogan "Just Bring It."

GLOSSARY

armored (AR-muhrd)—covered with metal to protect against attacks

blockbuster (BLOK-buhs-ter)—something that is very effective, successful, expensive, large, or extravagant

bout (BOWT)—a contest or trial of strength, such as a wrestling or boxing match

demi-god (DEM-ee-god)—a mythological being who is partly human and partly divine

destined (DES-tind)—meant to be or do something

franchise (FRAN-chize)—a series of films or TV shows that feature the same characters or follow a continuing storyline

gridiron (GRID-ahy-ern)—a football field marked with evenly spaced lines

grossing (GROHSS-ing)—earning or bringing in money

persona (per-SOH-nuh)—a character or personality

prequel (PREE-kwul)—a story about events that happen to characters before they appear in an existing story

trash-talking (TRASH-tawk-ing)—boastful talk used to intimidate opponents

READ MORE

Corrick, James A. *Dwayne "The Rock" Johnson*. Modern Role Models. Broomall, PA: Mason Crest, 2013.

Pantaleo, Steve. *WWE Ultimate Superstar Guide*. Indianapolis, In.: DK/BradyGames, 2015.

Ratner, Brett and Linda Sunshine. *The Art and Making of Hercules*. New York: HarperCollins Publishers, 2014.

INTERNET SITES

FactHound offers a safe, fun way to find Internet sites related to this book. All of the sites on FactHound have been researched by our staff.

Here's all you do:

Visit *www.facthound.com*

Type in this code: 9781515710967

Check out projects, games and lots more at
www.capstonekids.com

INDEX